AIR
FREIGHTERS

AIR FREIGHTERS

CLASSIC AMERICAN PROPS

Stephen Piercey,
Philip Wallick, David Oliver,
Austin J. Brown & Mark R. Wagner
Karl-Heinz Morawietz & Jörg Weier

MILITARY PRESS
New York

This 1990 edition published by
Military Press, New York, and
distributed by Crown Publishers, Inc.,
225 Park Avenue South, New York,
New York 10003.

© Osprey Publishing Limited

ISBN 0–517–01220–0

hgfedcba

Compiled, edited and designed by
Richard and Janette Widdows

Printed and bound in Hong Kong

[The material in this book previously
appeared in the Osprey Aerospace
publications *Sky Truck* and *Sky Truck 2*
(Stephen Piercey), *Fire Bombers* (Philip
Wallick), *Big Props* and *Miami Props* (Austin
J. Brown & Mark R. Wagner), *Alaskan Props*
(Karl-Heinz Morawietz & Jörg Weier) and
Bush Flying (David Oliver)]

CONTENTS

OPPOSITE Profile of a prop: one of the four Wright R-3350s that power Lockheed Super Constellation 1049, HI-207. [*Stephen Piercey*]

TITLE PAGE The pointed nose of a DC-6 fire tanker operating out of Chico, California. The black panel is found on most water bombers, an anti-dazzle device that makes it easier for the pilot to look ahead over the nose in brilliant sunshine. [*Philip Wallick*]

STEPHEN PIERCEY (*left*), whose pictures make the biggest contribution to this book, was the founder and editor of *Propliner*, a magazine he produced in his spare time. He was employed initially by the British aviation weekly *Flight International* as their photo librarian, but it was as *Flight*'s chief photographer that he met his tragic death at the age of 27 along with his pilot colleague Cliff Barnett when their Aztec cameraship was involved in a mid-air collision in May 1984.

Although he was never able to recollect transatlantic crossings by DC-7C and Britannia aircraft at the age of two, Stephen Piercey had been devoted to propeller-driven transport aircraft since the early 1960s. His earliest memory was of a Constellation on finals to London Airport. This interest had taken him across the world, and such was his love for these flying crocks that he traveled over half a million miles to seek them out. In pursuit of his unusual hobby Stephen Piercey made more than 150 flights aboard piston-engined aircraft – often in difficult circumstances – and on occasions was known to share trips, not

always willingly, with a strange assortment of animal and inanimate cargoes.

PHILIP WALLICK, balloonist and power-boat racer as well as aircraft buff, is a professional photographer based at Chico, California. His company offers a full range of specialist services including multi-media production, video production and air-to-air photography.

AUSTIN BROWN and **MARK WAGNER** have produced more 'big prop' titles in the Osprey Color Series than all other photographers combined. However, piston-engined and turboprop-powered transport aircraft represent only a small part of their huge stock of aviation subjects. Austin Brown flew DC-3s in the Caribbean with Air BVI in the 1970s before returning to the UK, where he established his Bristol-based Aviation Picture Library, and he continues to fly commercially as a freelance. Mark Wagner currently operates on an independent basis as a professional photographer.

KARL-HEINZ MORAWIETZ and **JÖRG WEIER** grew up near Düsseldorf International Airport in West Germany and they have always had a special interest in old piston-engined airliners. Both have traveled extensively in Canada and Latin America to capture many memorable images of what are inevitably a diminishing breed of aircraft. Karl-Heinz Morawietz is a professional designer with an advertising agency and Jörg Weier works for a leading German airline.

DAVID OLIVER is the editor of Air Forces Monthly – required reading for every military aviation enthusiast. Initially a motorsport photographer, he switched to aviation subjects in the early 1980s.

BELOW Squatting on a ramp in northern Quebec with thousands of gallons of chemicals in her cabin tanks, this Constellation 749 is ready to begin her day's work at six in the morning spraying spruce budworm. The four to six-week spraying season results in millions of acres of forest being treated. [*Stephen Piercey*]

BOEING
B-17 Flying
Fortress

RIGHT Air Tanker No 09, seen at Chester, California as late as 1976, was one of those with a metal nose which followed the contours of the original, even to the extent of having a 'bombardier' panel. The slightly bulged belly tank, occupying the lower part of the former bomb bay, can just be seen. It was common to start a day hauling 1600 US gallons and switch to 1800 if all went well. [*Philip Wallick*]

BELOW This B-17 ended up with a moulded Plexiglas nose reminiscent of the wartime B-17F. Virtually all the air tanker Flying Fortresses had been B-17Gs, and in the conversion had gained totally new nose sections as well as major modifications elsewhere.
[*Philip Wallick*]

ABOVE The Boeing B-17 was the greatest and most famous of the early postwar former warbirds to serve in the tanker role. The red dye was added to the Phos-chek or Fire-trol water mix for high visibility, especially on the ground. [*Philip Wallick*]

BELOW A B-17 of Aero Union lets go its load of about 1800 US gallons on a fire at Paradise, California (near the Chico Air Attack Base) in 1971. The fire is out of picture to the right. [*Philip Wallick*]

LEFT Front end of one of a very large number of B-17 fire-bomber tankers. While the wartime exploits of the famous Fortress have filled dozens of published books, not much has been written about the type's postwar tanker role – yet individual B-17s flew more hours as tankers than they did as bombers. Fire-bombing is hard work and usually involves flying from dawn to dusk – sometimes for days on end if a really big fire takes hold. This venerable Flying Fortress and its crew have earned the welcome respite. [*Philip Wallick*]

BELOW LEFT Tails of fire-bombers awaiting call at Chico. All had the so-called Cheyenne tail turret, introduced with the final production batches (B-17G-90-BO, -50-DL and -55-VE), which reduced overall length by five inches. Ship 18 retains the gunner's transparent panels. In the background is a Grumman S-2 Tracker. [*Philip Wallick*]

BELOW Tail-on view of Chico fire-bomber No 19, whose aluminum skin over the former tail gunner's position warns 'Full when light goes out'. This particular fire tanker looked more like a transport than a bomber, resembling the C-108, CB-17 and local transport rebuilds in Sweden and Indo-China. The streamlining made no significant difference to fire-bomber performance. The aircraft has been as far as possible restored to wartime standard and is on display at Castle Air Force Base Museum, California. The slits behind the engines are cooling air exits. [*Philip Wallick*]

BOEING B-17 FLYING FORTRESS

Starting engines at Redding, California, in 1976. The
Fort was universally liked, being generally regarded
as flying like an enlarged Piper Cub; but its rock-like
stability could be a problem near the fire.
[*Philip Wallick*]

BOEING B-17 FLYING FORTRESS

BELOW Aero Union No 17 about to touch down at Chester. With its totally manual controls, the B-17 had to be manouvered with muscle power, though in turns it had an odd tendency to overbank and sometimes in desperation the pilot would close down the engines on the high wing to try to bring it

down. Near the airfield it was difficult to lose speed until the ASI had fallen to the flap limit of 142 mph. [*Philip Wallick*]

BOTTOM Tanker 17 landing at Chester for a reload in 1975. The dust clearly shows the aerodynamics of the

wings, which are still creating lift and tip vortices. To modern pilots this big taildragger posed unexpected problems in its tendency to swing (swap ends on take-off or landing). With a crosswind the pilot really had to earn his pay. [*Philip Wallick*]

BELOW Port pair of R-1820 Cyclones en route to the fire. The engines retained their GE turbo-superchargers, making for excellent performance under high-altitude conditions. The propellers were 11 ft 7 in Hamilton Standards. [*Philip Wallick*]

LEFT Bill Waldman in the left seat of Tanker No 17 of Aero Union. Everyone liked having a co-pilot, especially one who could do the mundane chores of washing, oiling and endlessly checking such things as the retardant load and center of gravity position. Take-off was a two-man job, the non-flying pilot reading out manifold pressure and airspeed and working the gear and flaps. [*Philip Wallick*]

RIGHT Major maintenance in the Aero Union hangar at Chico in preparation for the 1975 season. This particular B-17 has a streamlined nose but retains the projecting balconies for the hand-aimed cheek guns, which were added along with the chin turret to provide the greatest possible firepower against head-on attack. [*Philip Wallick*]

BELOW RIGHT Another view of maintenance before the start of the 1975 season. The bomb doors are open, as they are in most fire-bomber conversions during release of retardant. During the summer fire season the days were so busy that maintenance had to be done at night. [*Philip Wallick*]

BELOW The fire-bomber B-17s converted with many kinds of locally contrived modification to replace the wartime turrets, the most noticeable differences being in the nose. Ship 19, seen operating with Aero Union from Chester, California, was one of the ones with a pointed aluminum nose. Pilot and co-pilot normally went aboard through the open door, reaching up with both arms and swinging their legs up and inside. [*Philip Wallick*]

BOEING B-17 FLYING FORTRESS

Aero Union No 19 parked at sunset in 1971, with
No 1 propeller feathered. Considering the enormous
total of hours flown by the B-17 tankers the accident
record was commendable. [*Philip Wallick*]

BELOW The handsomely finished Black Hills No 89. In the background is the Aero Union hangar at Chester, California, and part of the fire-retardant tank farm can be seen between the main gears. Most civil Forts were previously operated as the fire-bombers until a Forest Service directive stated that the planes were too old for such hazardous operations. This released the bombers for sale to warbird enthusiasts but, unfortunately, many perfectly fine and flyable civilian B-17s went to the Air Force, where they now rot outside as gate guardians at the various bases that are part of the USAF Museum's heritage program. [*Philip Wallick*]

RIGHT Thirty inches manifold . . . airborne, gear up. Black Hills No 89 gets away at Chester in the hot summer of 1976. The B-17 was always popular, but with 1800 gallons pilots normally felt they had a choice of climbing straight ahead or making a turn and losing height – but not of turning and climbing at the same time. [*Philip Wallick*]

BELOW No 89 starting engines before a firefighting mission. The row of retardant storage tanks can be seen in the background, together with the landing gears of a DC-6, a considerably more powerful tanker able to put down a heavier load. [*Philip Wallick*]

LEFT Black Hills Aviation's home base is Alamagordo, New Mexico. From this angle the projecting bay doors under the retardant tank can be seen clearly. Normal payload is 1600 US gallons. [*Philip Wallick*]

BELOW LEFT The last bomber, parked in the sunshine at Mesa. Note the remarkable array of avionics antennas, and the stencilled 'MAX LD 16250 LBS, 1805 GALS'. [*Philip Wallick*]

BELOW A picture taken at Mesa, Arizona in 1984, showing one of the last B-17s to remain active – almost 50 years after the B-17's first flight at Seattle and 40 years after the first flight of this particular example. Throughout, the old bomber's structure never gave a moment's real worry. The worst problems, to a pilot familiar with the type, was its stability. [*Philip Wallick*]

BELOW This old Boeing B-17 Flying Fortress was not kept operational in Bolivia as a historic memorial to the war, but was flown commercially. Operated by Frigorificos Reyes, CP-891 was the last of the cargo B-17s. Flying from La Paz, she eventually earned long overdue retirement in a USAF museum in California. The development of Model 299, as it was called by Boeing, into the definitive war-wagon that lumbered across the German skies in 1944–45, took almost a decade, the prototype taking off for the first time on 28 July 1935. The ultimate Fortress, the B-17G, did not find its way to front-line squadrons until September 1943, no less than five sub-types preceding it. [*Stephen Piercey*]

RIGHT A local Bolivian girl at La Paz in company with a flock of sheep and a Flying Fortress. The mighty B-17 was perhaps the strongest symbol of America's military effort against the Axis power in Europe. A total of 12,751 Flying Fortresses eventually took to the skies – of which more than a third were lost in combat – but unlike its fellow heavy-hauler of the European theater, the B-24 Liberator, it is still found in some numbers. [*Stephen Piercey*]

Top left Beefy Boeing: Flying Fortress meat wagon CP-891 taxies in to her base at La Paz, stirring up clouds of dust in the process. Two of her crew served on B-17s in the last war, and who could have believed that they would still be flying the aeroplane nearly 40 years later? [*Stephen Piercey*]

Left Laden with general cargo for Trinidad, Bolivia, the Flying Fortress departs for the second time in a busy day. [*Stephen Piercey*]

Top Bolivian mechanics show more interest in the foreigner than their work. A few problems were rectified on No 4 engine before a late morning flight. [*Stephen Piercey*]

Above At a distant meat farm in Santiago, 100 miles east of San José de Chiquitos, in eastern Bolivia, the B-17 is loaded with slaughtered cattle destined for markets in La Paz. One may be misled into believing that Frigorificos Reyes has refrigeration units in its aircraft (or at its base); readers may be assured that there were no such facilities. [*Stephen Piercey*]

BOEING B-17 FLYING FORTRESS

Loaded with 7000 lb of chopped cattle, this old Flying Fortress barely cleared the tops of the Bolivian Cordilleras near Choquecamata on her return from Santiago with a freshly slaughtered catch in 1977. At an altitude of 17,500 feet over the mountains her crew and one passenger took turns to make use of any oxygen bottle and air-pipe. [*Stephen Piercey*]

BOEING C-97 Strato-freighter

RIGHT This former USAF C-97G Stratofreighter N297HP, operated by Hawkins & Powers of Greybull, Wyoming, waits at King Salmon Airport for a trip back to Anchorage fully loaded with salmon. [*Karl-Heinz Morawietz/Jörg Weier*]

BELOW The C-97G's temperamental, maintenance-hog and occasionally pyrotechnic 3500 hp Pratt & Whitney R-4360-59 Wasp Majors thrumming along on top on 9 July 1983, when N297HP made three return flights between Anchorage International and King Salmon. [*Karl-Heinz Morawietz/Jörg Weier*]

BOEING C-97 STRATOFREIGHTER

BELOW This Boeing KC-97, registered N854OD, probably last saw military service with an Air National Guard Unit, and since then must have been up to no good before being caught and stored in the Fort Lauderdale Customs' long-term parking area. [*Austin J. Brown/Mark R. Wagner*]

ABOVE Flying fish. In the months of June and July millions of salmon return from the open sea to spawn in Alaskan waters. It's a lucrative time for fishermen – and for the cargo companies who ferry their catch from small airfields along the coastline to the fish processing plants at Anchorage and Kodiak Island in the Gulf of Alaska. [*Karl Heinz Morawietz/Jörg Weier*]

BOEING C-97 STRATOFREIGHTER

BELOW Every aircraft in this picture has been impounded by US Customs and reside here at Hollywood Airport, Fort Lauderdale, awaiting their fate. With all its four props feathered, the KC-97 is unlikely to experience any Florida fun this summer! [*Austin J. Brown/Mark R. Wagner*]

BELOW, MAIN PICTURE Just past the 'piano keys', HI-468 flashes past the United ramp at Miami. [*Austin J. Brown/Mark R. Wagner*]

BELOW, INSET Just a foot or so above the runway the Strat almost flares and eventually impresses everyone with an incredibly smooth nosewheel-first touchdown. [*Austin J. Brown/Mark R. Wagner*]

RIGHT Operators from the Dominican Republic add cosmopolitan interest to the big prop scene at MIA. Agro Air operates two Boeing C-97G Stratofreighters and a DC-8 on behalf of Aerochago and Aeromar. Here, with full flaps extended, HI-468 pitches its nose down on the final approach to 27 left. [*Austin J. Brown/Mark R. Wagner*]

ABOVE Almost certainly the only surviving Boeing 377 Stratocruiser, N74603 resides at Tucson International Airport. Bought by Aero Spacelines of Van Nuys, California, as a source of spares for its famous Guppy conversion program, the Strat remained largely intact until it became a repository for aircraft parts after the tail was removed in 1982. Boeing only built a limited edition of 50 'Statuscruisers' and N74603 was one of a batch of ten delivered to Northwest Airlines. [*Stephen Piercey*]

ABOVE RIGHT A small number of surplus military Boeing C-97s have arrived on the civil scene in America. Powered by massive Pratt & Whitney R-4360 engines of 3500 hp, this example may occasionally be found in Alaska hauling oil or fish. She was auctioned in Arizona during 1980 as 'lot 64'. [*Stephen Piercey*]

RIGHT Aero Spacelines' Super Guppy 201, F-BPPA, is operated by Aeromaritime and spends most of its time ferrying Airbus parts from Britain and West Germany to the final assembly building in Toulouse. Based on the C-97J version of the Boeing Stratocruiser, the Super Guppy 201 is powered by 4912 ehp Allison 501-D22Cs and first flew on 24 August 1970. Vital statistics include a height of 48 ft 6 in, length of 143 ft 10 in, and a maximum take-off weight of 170,000 lb; economical cruising speed is a stately 250 mph at 20,000 feet. [*Austin J. Brown/Mark R. Wagner*]

CONSOLIDATED
Privateer

LEFT Remarkably few B-24 Liberators ever served as fire-fighting bombers. This very unusual variant was formerly a P4Y-2G of the US Coast Guard, rebuilt with circular (instead of vertical ellipse) engine cowls, housing Wright R-2600 engines of 1700 hp from B-25s, and with many other changes. The observer nose was peculiar to this rare Coast Guard model. [*Philip Wallick*]

BELOW This view shows well the engine installation, which bears no relation to anything originally fitted to any P4Y-2G, PB4Y-2 or B-24! Note the steps up the side of the fuselage. [*Philip Wallick*]

CONSOLIDATED PRIVATEER

BELOW Another view of the converted P4Y-2G, which itself was a much-modified derivative of the Navy PB4Y-2 Privateer, which in turn was a gross redesign of a late-model B-24. The tail is broadly similar to that of the PB4Y-2 Privateer, apart from having no turret and greatly enlarged side observer stations (the Privateer had smaller projecting blisters, which originally carried guns). The tail was similar to that of the Liberator C.IX and RY-3, but not the same as that of the final production bomber, the B-24N. [*Philip Wallick*]

ABOVE Cockpit of the P4Y-2G, with a bonedome resting on the left control-wheel shaft. In World War 2 the Liberator family were second only to the B-29 as being the most complex and demanding production aircraft. [*Philip Wallick*]

RIGHT Room with a view: the giant waist observer windows of the former Coast Guard aircraft almost made one wonder what was holding the tail on. This view is looking forward, past what in other versions would have been the bomb-bay and on to the cockpit. [*Philip Wallick*]

Top left Just getting airborne at Chester is the last surviving operational PB4Y-2 Privateer, which like the P4Y-2G previously described originally stemmed from the B-24 Liberator program. Also like the former Coast Guard aircraft, this Privateer has been rebuilt with much more powerful B-25 engines in circular engine cowlings. [*Philip Wallick*]

Above Here the surviving PB4Y-2 (operated by Hawkins & Powers) is just beginning to tuck away its gear, the giant single wheels swinging out and up to lie in recesses in the thin wings. All the single-fin members of the family not only had better control than the mass produced twin-fin aircraft but reduced drag too. The PB4Y also had a dihedral horizontal stabilizer on the tailplane. [*Philip Wallick*]

Left Hawkins & Powers' rare Privateer parked on the ramp at Chandler Airfield, Arizona, in February 1984. 'Bomb doors' agape, this converted PB4Y-2 can haul 2000 US gal (18,250 lb) of fire-retardant borate. [*Stephen Piercey*]

CONSOLIDATED PRIVATEER

The PB4Y was first used in the fire-bomber role in 1959. It could carry 2000 US gallons, and dump it on a fire all at once. This was the first time anything like this kind of knockout blow had been possible. A little earlier, during tests at Ramona, in southern California, a Boeing YC-97 had been used with 4000-gallon capacity, but it could only put down 1000 at a time. [*Stephen Piercey*]

BELOW Touching down at Chester, the PB4Y-2 shows in side view the oil coolers hung under the rear of each engine nacelle. In the original aircraft the oil radiators were tucked away in ducts inside the deep vertical-ellipse cowlings. The life of a fire-bomber is hard, operating consistently at high power in hot summer air at low level – to say nothing of flying through the fire. [*Philip Wallick*]

RIGHT Here the PB4Y-2 has its take-off flap selected, but the gear is fully retracted. Unlike the B-24 bombers these aircraft never had turbosuperchargers, since high-altitude performance was unimportant. But despite high weights and a much higher wing loading the PB4Y had better climb than the B-17 and was considerably more manouverable. This aircraft has the nose of an early B-24D or PB4Y-1 spliced on, replacing the PB4Y-2's bulbous gun turret. [*Philip Wallick*]

CONVAIR 340, 440, 580 & 600

A brush fire rages through the airfield boundary behind a Convair 440 Metropolitan at St Croix in April 1980. Light aircraft were rescued, but horses at the nearby racecourse stampeded when the flames overwhelmed their stables. The shuttle service between St Thomas and St Croix in the US Virgin Islands is run by American Inter-Island, a subsidiary of American Airlines, with five 440s operating the route. After the disastrous crash of an American Boeing 727 in a landing accident at St Thomas in the mid-1970s, the carrier refused to fly jets into St Croix until the airfield at St Thomas was improved. [*Austin J. Brown/Mark R. Wagner*]

ABOVE LEFT Sedalia-Marshall-Boonville Stageline Inc of Dallas, Texas, own this Convair 600. Converted from a 1948 Convair 240-0, the 600 is powered by two Rolls-Royce Dart 542-4 turboprop engines. Leased from SMB to a Miami-based operator during early 1988, N74850 is one of nearly 20 Dart-powered CV600 and 640s in SMB's fleet.

LEFT A view through the terrace garden at Beauvais, France, during Paris *Salon* week. Visiting aircraft such as Nor-Fly's 440 are not allowed to land at the show and Beauvais, some 80 miles north of Paris, is a favorite alternative.

BELOW LEFT Southern Express of Miami operate this Convair 440 with a fleet of Navajos and Bandeirantes.

ABOVE XA-LOU began life in September 1953 as the KLM Convairliner 340 *Nicholaas Maes*, being transfered to ALM Dutch Antillean Airlines ten years later. Following a brief spell on the US register, she was sold to Aviateca in 1970, after which she was operated by Aerotur from Cancun in Mexico. When this photograph was taken in March 1985 the aircraft was in open storage at Opa Locka, Florida.

BELOW Spit and polish! This immaculate US Navy VC-131F was one of a batch of 36 R4Y-1s manufactured between June 1955 and May 1956, and was approaching its 30th birthday when this picture was taken at Barbados in March 1985.

[Photographs by Austin J. Brown/Mark R. Wagner]

CONVAIR 440

BELOW Pictured in March 1985, this Convair 440 was built for Swissair as HB-IMN and first flew on 13 March 1957, named *Zug*. It was acquired by Pan Adria of Yugoslavia in 1969 and then sold in 1976 after a period of storage to Associated Products of America. One of the Convair's original competitors, a Martin 4-0-4, can be seen in the background among a line-up of business aircraft.
[*Austin J. Brown/Mark R. Wagner*]

BELOW Norsk Metropolitan Klubb's Convair 440 pictured at West Malling in Kent after a warbirds show, capturing the atmosphere of an overcast English day. An ex-SAS machine, this must be one of the most ambitious preservation projects yet to keep an airliner flying; but due to the restrictions on airworthiness, it was up for sale at the time of going to press. [*Austin J. Brown/Mark R. Wagner*]

BOTTOM Sunbird Air, based on the National Jet ramp at FTL, operate two Convair 440s. N411GA wears a dark blue and yellow livery, while N26DR is red and purple. [*Austin J. Brown/Mark R. Wagner*]

OPPOSITE, TOP Until it ceased operations on 18 January 1986, Seair Alaska provided passenger services between Anchorage and communities such as Aniak, Bethel and St Mary's, using DHC-6 Twin Otter and Convair CV-580 turboprops, including N5822. [*Karl-Heinz Morawietz/Jörg Weier*]

TOP Prinair purchased four Convair 580s in 1981–82. N589PL, in a hybrid scheme, lifts off from St Thomas in the Virgin Islands.
[*Austin J. Brown/Mark R. Wagner*]

ABOVE An experimentally registered Convair 580 of the National Research Council of Canada at Juliana Airport on St Maarten in the Leeward Islands in December 1981. Originally a Model 440, the turbine conversion was carried out for owner Bethlehem Steel in 1965. [*Austin J. Brown/Mark R. Wagner*]

LEFT Confirmed Convair of The Way International, a biblical foundation from New Knoxville, Ohio, visited Bristol during its mission to Britain in the late 1970s. A 580 converted from a Model 340, it started life with United Airlines in 1952.
[*Austin J. Brown/Mark R. Wagner*]

CURTISS C-46 Commando

In the rarified 13,000 foot-high atmosphere of La Paz, Bolivia, the highest capital city in the world, you really do have to trust in God and Pratt & Whitney if you're flying a Curtiss C-46 Commando. With 2000 hp of tired iron turning on either side, CP-974 *Super Raton* ('Super Mouse') is held against the brakes while the pilot checks for any tell-tale mag drop. The single-engined performance of a C-46 is less than sparkling – you don't climb, you don't maintain height, you just head earthwards. The Commando in the background belongs to Empresa Transportes Aereos Ltda. [*Stephen Piercey*]

LEFT Kicking up some dust, CP-974 taxies out for take-off. When this picture was taken in April 1984, CP-974 was operated by meat-hauler Empresa Transportes Aereos Ltda. The aircraft is festooned with a variety of aerials for direction finding and communications. [*Stephen Piercey*]

RIGHT Synchronicity: *Super Raton's* R-2800-34s ping into life and start to hit that perfect beat. You can almost hear it . . . [*Stephen Piercey*]

BELOW Resplendent in its polished, natural metal finish, the broad-shouldered Commando bounds across a rudimentary taxiway. Maintenance is carried out in the open as a matter of routine – hangarage is a luxury most Bolivian operators cannot afford or don't need, and probably both. [*Stephen Piercey*]

CURTISS C-46 COMMANDO

BELOW Downtime for CP-1244, member of the Empresa Transportes Aereos Ltda fleet operating out of La Paz. The Pink Panther seems to be impersonating Noel Coward – and you need the same *sangfroid* to work ageing piston-engined airplanes in South America. [*Stephen Piercey*]

BOTTOM Cargo Curtiss Commandos and passenger Viscounts comprise the fleet of Aeropesca, a small established Colombian carrier. C-46 HK-388, seen at its Bogota base, went missing on a flight from Medellin to Barranquilla in October 1981. She was later found abandoned floating in the River Orteguaza, in south-west Colombia. The old Commando had been hijacked by left-wing guerrillas who forced the crew to fly to Panama, where crates of arms were loaded. [*Stephen Piercey*]

BELOW In April 1984 Transportes Aereos Universal Ltda operated two Commandos, but CP-1588 was subsequently written off after an accident. Large chunks of the aircraft were still cloistered around Universal's premises at La Paz in May 1985. Bolivia suffers from a high rate of illiteracy, so the motif on the fin may have a serious purpose. [*Stephen Piercey*]

BOTTOM Bolivia could not exist without its faithful Curtiss Commandos. Written off with great regularity, these old World War 2 workhorses are either rebuilt or replaced by other C-46s that can be bought at knock-down prices from South or North America. Sole fleet member of Transportes Aereos San Martin (TASMA) flies from La Paz, Bolivia, and was seen departing from its base in 1977. Within 30 minutes she was back on the ramp after suffering a blown engine on take-off. [*Stephen Piercey*]

LEFT AND BELOW Universal's surviving C-46, CP-1655, tops up with oil and gasoline at Espiritu in April 1984. The old Commando has since been resprayed in a smart livery. [*Stephen Piercey*]

BOTTOM A few years ago LACSA of Costa Rica still flew two pristine C-46s on domestic passenger services. TI-LRB *Chorotega* was seen at the lovely coastal town of Golfito. [*Stephen Piercey*]

ABOVE Empresa Transportes Aereos Ltda is one of about a dozen meat-haulers which operate out of La Paz. Framed by a snow-sprinkled peak rising from the *altiplano*, a C-46 stands with its cargo door held open. [*Stephen Piercey*]

RIGHT Another of the faithful Commandos, CP-1593, comes home after foraging in the Bolivian hinterland. [*Stephen Piercey*]

LEFT The Commando is a big airplane, a dominating 21 feet 8 inches tall, 78 feet 4 inches long and with a wingspan of exactly 108 feet. It must have seemed huge when the civil CW-20 first flew in March 1940. The demands of war left no room for the manufacture of commercial models; 3141 examples of the military C-46 were completed when production ceased in 1945. [*Stephen Piercey*]

BELOW The equipment might be old, but it's paid for and a good deal more practical than alternative forms of Bolivian transportation, with road and rail development hamstrung by national poverty and awesome natural obstacles. [*Stephen Piercey*]

CURTISS C-46 COMMANDO

BELOW After a disastrous start the C-46 became a hero of the 'Hump', the China airlift over the Himalayas from Burma and India in World War 2. Old-timers who flew the C-46 along the route back in 1943–45 will probably appreciate the airmanship of this Commando crew as they gain altitude to clear the Andes. CP-1593 was photographed from the flight-deck of another Commando, CP-754. [*Stephen Piercey*]

ABOVE Working out of La Paz, this C-46 picks up a cargo from a remote farm in the Bolivian lowlands. Frigorifico Santa Rita operate two Commandos, CP-754 (pictured) and CP-1848. A lone DC-3 (CP-529) is also in its inventory. Down on the farm, a specially adapted ox-cart is used to reach the cargo door. Bolivia is not a major beef producer like Brazil or Argentina – most of its livestock consists of sheep and goats. [*Stephen Piercey*]

RIGHT A safer, more substantial walkway was employed for a second batch of slaughtered animals. [*Stephen Piercey*]

BELOW Well worn, CP-754 exudes rugged dependability. The wide track landing gear and generous flap area are vital for survival on strips consisting of grass, dust or gravel. [*Stephen Piercey*]

LEFT Wings clipped forever, a C-46 waits for the *coup de grâce* at La Paz behind an intact CAMBA Martin 4-0-4, CP-1570. [*Stephen Piercey*]

RIGHT An ex-Luftwaffe F-4 front-seater is the chief pilot of Eldorado Ltda, an outfit which consists solely of this one C-46 Commando, CP-1617. [*Stephen Piercey*]

BELOW Typically Bolivian: peasants' washing hangs out at El Alto Airport in La Paz, strung across the cargo area. A pair of Transportes Aereos Bolivar C-46s undergo some form of maintenance outside the airline's corporate headquarters. [*Stephen Piercey*]

CURTISS C-46 COMMANDO

Nose riding high at La Paz in November 1977, Commando *Junia* continues to fly with Servicios Aereos Bolivianos despite a number of serious crashes (and subsequent rebuilds) in which aircrew have been killed. Some say that her construction plate is probably the only original part. [*Stephen Piercey*]

LEFT Although LANICA no longer exists, its successor Aeronica is still believed to fly this C-46, AN-BRG, on domestic passenger services within Nicaragua. This beautiful relic was seen at Puerto Cabezas on the eastern coast of Nicaragua during a fuel stop. [*Stephen Piercey*]

RIGHT Unusual attitude for AN-BRG landing at Bluefields, Nicaragua. Loaded with 50 passengers, the packed Commando had just completed six sectors from Managua and was scheduled for two more before the day was out. The airstrips leave a lot to be desired, and several serious accidents have been known to occur. [*Stephen Piercey*]

BELOW The same aircraft visited Waspam on its weekly 'tour' around the country, the airfield being home to a large herd of cattle. Here she is boarded by a group of English Jehovah's Witnesses. [*Stephen Piercey*]

CURTISS C-46 COMMANDO

Northland Air Manitoba, formally Ilford-Riverton
Airways, operates cargo services in northern
Manitoba and the Arctic with Curtiss Commandos.
Powered by two 2000 hp Pratt & Whitney R-2800
radials, the 45-year-old C-46 can carry a useful
16,000-lb load of freight. [*David Oliver*]

LEFT The bulbous shape of C-GIXZ stands on the Air Manitoba ramp with its cargo doors open. Note the tracked loading trolly parked under the wing. [*David Oliver*]

BELOW The early morning sunshine shows up the polished metal finish of C-GIXZ. The C-46 is parked in front of Air Manitoba's freight sheds at Winnipeg Airport. More than 100 of the 3160 Commandos built during World War 2 remain active in North and South America. [*David Oliver*]

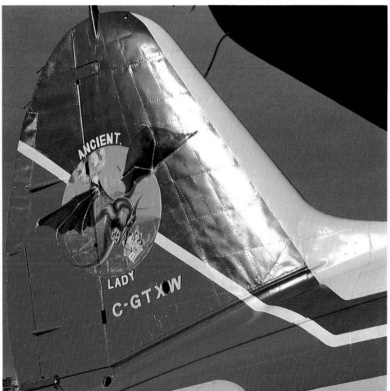

TOP LEFT Air Manitoba operates one of the largest fleets of C-46 freighters in North America.

TOP CF-FNC, a well-weathered Air Manitoba C-46F Commando freighter, follows a Perimeter DC-3 out to Winnipeg's main runway in November 1987.

LEFT AND ABOVE C-GTXW *Ancient Lady*, delivered in October 1987, is the latest addition to the airline's fleet of four Commandos. Here she is nearing the end of an extensive rebuild at Winnipeg.
[*Photographs by David Oliver*]

LEFT Not too many Curtiss C-46 Commandos still fly in the far north. Fairbanks-based Cliff Everts bought this snow-encrusted example from the Japanese Air Self-Defense Force, whose faded Dayglo trim it still bore when photographed at Anchorage International in the winter of 1982.
[*Karl-Heinz Morawietz/Jörg Weier*]

BELOW Many C-46s are still active. They offer a generous payload and the type remains competitive, though poor single-engine performance has caused many a ditching. This natural metal C-46, N1807M, has changed hands many times, but remains based out of Miami's Corrosion Corner. [*Stephen Piercey*]

LEFT The C-46's cockpit was the original 'flying greenhouse'. From its multi-faceted windows a 'Dumbo' pilot can (in one respect at least) look down on drivers of more modern machinery such as Boeing 727s. Note the half-moon controls and massive trim wheels. Mmm . . . you can almost smell the sweat-stained leather, oil, avgas, hydraulic fluid and stale stodgy smoke. Pure nostalgia. If you could bottle it, you'd make a fortune among big props buffs.
[*Karl-Heinz Morawietz/Jörg Weier*]

DOUGLAS
DC-3 Dakota

LEFT Eastern Express's DC-3A on finals to land on the cross runway at Miami.
[*Austin J. Brown/Mark R. Wagner*]

BELOW N34PB reloads with passengers at Key West Airport. The aircraft operated into Miami for years sporting the Provincetown–Boston logo until their takeover by Texas Air Corporation.
[*Austin J. Brown/Mark R. Wagner*]

ABOVE DC-3 N92578 was found hiding in the evening shadows at Fort Lauderdale Executive Airport. The Dakota legend really began with the DST (Douglas Sleeper Transport), certificated on 21 May 1936. Interestingly, the original DST layout featured a separate berth for honeymoon couples, but the idea was discarded before the airplane entered service. Pity... [*Austin J. Brown/Mark R. Wagner*]

LEFT Fancy an Air Adventure? Then contact the company at Fort Lauderdale's Hollywood Airport for a whirl in their attractive passenger-carrying DC-3. [*Austin J. Brown/Mark R. Wagner*]

ABOVE LEFT Next to the Air Adventure machine, in the north-east corner of FTL, was N47CR, another pretty DC-3. The four chimneys on top of the fuselage were not, as far as we know, a factory-fitted option on the standard model Dakota. [*Austin J. Brown/Mark R. Wagner*]

RIGHT An ex-Millardair DC-3 registered as N87664 parked at Opa Locka Airport next to DC-6 N843TA. [*Austin J. Brown/Mark R. Wagner*]

BELOW As one Opa Locka Airport worker exclaimed, 'Everything on this goddam airport is for sale – except me!' [*Austin J. Brown/Mark R. Wagner*]

LEFT DC-3A EI-AYO is now safe in the Science Museum's hangar near Swindon, England, after retrieval from open storage at Shannon, Eire, in 1978. Originally NC16071, it served with United Air Lines from 1936 until 1954. United had specified 1200 hp Pratt & Whitney R-1830-92 Twin Wasp radials to give the DC-3 enough power to fly routes over the Rockies with a fair safety margin. [*Stephen Piercey*]

ABOVE AND LEFT N230F pauses for reflection. The DC-3 celebrated its 50th birthday in December 1985 and the world's most famous transport airplane still seems as irreplaceable as ever. [*Stephen Piercey*]

TOP Aptly titled DC-3s and Convair 440s served points in the sunshine state of Florida with Air Sunshine during the 1970s. Absorbed by Air Florida in 1979, the airline offered bargain $50 day trips to Disneyworld from Miami by one of its friendly 36-seat Daks – satisfaction guaranteed. [*Stephen Piercey*]

DOUGLAS DC-3 DAKOTA

The Hill Air Company ramp at Fort Lauderdale International is full of interesting specimens. When photographed the 'Budget Rent-a-Plane' DC-3, HI-445, had recently been gainfully employed in the motion picture *Police Academy 5*. From a distance it looks a bit of a heap, but closer inspection reveals that all the oil stains are in fact painted on. The airplane is in very good health having recently received an engine cannibalized from N3753N. In the movie, the DC-3 flies to the Bahamas with pigs, goats, chickens – and 22 toilet seats. [*Austin J. Brown/Mark R. Wagner*]

DOUGLAS DC-3 DAKOTA

BELOW Luridly painted with images of Mexico, this wild Gooney was used for charters by a travel club out of Fort Lauderdale in the late 1970s.
[*Austin J. Brown/Mark R. Wagner*]

BOTTOM Somewhat squatter than usual, this poor DC-3 ran through the hedge at the upwind end of St Vincent's cul-de-sac runway at Arnos Vale Airport in early 1985.
[*Austin J. Brown/Mark R. Wagner*]

RIGHT Island trader: one of many Dakotas that ply their trade around the Caribbean islands is the San Juan-based, wheel-spatted N80617. Flying with St Maarten Traders, she was hauling fish to Tortola in the British Virgin Islands during March 1980.
[*Stephen Piercey*]

Above Like a tired dog resting its head on someone's knee, Top Flight's Dakota G-ANAF peers over the top of G-AMHJ's rear fuselage. They were both in the pound at Exeter, England in November 1986 when the company sadly went into receivership. [*Austin J. Brown/Mark R. Wagner*]

Top Benign mountains provide the backdrop for a pair of Air BVI DC-3s on Beef Island Airport in 1980. VP-LVH (foreground) is the grand old lady of what must have been the world's most immaculate DC-3 fleet. 'Hotel was built at Santa Monica in July 1937 for American Airlines as *Flagship Philadelphia*, and co-author Austin Brown was at the wheel when she clocked up 65,000 flight hours on 14 June 1979.

Above The front office of VP-LVH, but can a picture communicate the feel of this wonderful machine? [*Photographs by Austin J. Brown/Mark R. Wagner*]

ABOVE This otherwise immaculate DC-3 of Bo-S-Air bears the familiar scars of a landing gear collapse at Charlotte, North Carolina, in March 1985.
[*Austin J. Brown/Mark R. Wagner*]

DOUGLAS DC-3 DAKOTA

ABOVE LEFT N102AP's sister ship, in complimentary colors, parked on a rare rainy day at St Thomas. This standard C-47A has missed out on the panoramic passenger window modification.
[*Austin J. Brown/Mark R. Wagner*]

LEFT That C-47's a C-53. Built as the troop-carrying version of the faithful old Dak, it had no provision for heavy cargo and only a small passenger door. Flown by Aero Virgin Islands of St Thomas on routes between the islands and San Juan, it was eventually withdrawn from service in the early 1980s.
[*Austin J. Brown/Mark R. Wagner*]

ABOVE What a beautiful paint job. Virgin Islands International Airways' DC-3-201D combines the hibiscus flower with the natural colors of the islands. N102AP was built for Eastern Airlines in September 1940 and the old girl is still as eager as ever.
[*Austin J. Brown/Mark R. Wagner*]

LEFT For many years two COPA Dakotas linked Bocas del Toro, Changuinola and David with Panama City. [*Stephen Piercey*]

BELOW Despite the introduction of new equipment (HS.748s, for example), SATENA's fleet of DC-3s and C-47s continue to perform the vital social service of providing a reliable link between the industrialized areas of Colombia and its underdeveloped rural regions. The port engine of this C-47 (FAC 1120) comes under scrutiny during a turnround check. [*Stephen Piercey*]

LEFT *Taxi Aéreo*: DC-3 HK-329 of El Venado pauses between operations at Villavicencio, Colombia, in October 1977. [*Stephen Piercey*]

ABOVE Four Star Air Cargo C-47B takes a breather in the shadow of the mountain which has brought so much disaster to St Thomas, either by aircraft hitting it or by influencing the winds which produce so much shear on finals. In 1985, three C-47s operated alongside two Beech 18s and a DC-6A leased from Trans-Air-Link. [*Austin J. Brown/Mark R. Wagner*]

DOUGLAS DC-3 DAKOTA

Guatemala's Aviateca flies a fleet of DC-3s on domestic services. TG-ATA was a casualty in 1978 when she crashed into a swamp near Flores.
[*Stephen Piercey*]

DOUGLAS DC-3 DAKOTA

RIGHT One of Northland Air Manitoba's four DC-3s at the Winnipeg holding point. C-FIKD was delivered to the RAF as KP266 in 1945 and following a recent rebuild was fitted with panoramic rear windows. The Dakotas fly to a number of Indian Reservations with such names as Red Sucker Lake, Garden Hill, God's River and God's Lake Narrows. Behind is Perimeter's C-FFAY, a 1942-built DC-3. [*David Oliver*]

BELOW Air Cargo America's C-47B N10801 pauses a moment beside Caribou N544Y at San Juan International in November 1979. Beautifully polished, both aircraft delivered light cargo down-island into airfields that were too small for the big jets. The C-47 had previously served with the West German Luftwaffe for many years as CA + 014. [*Austin J. Brown/Mark R. Wagner*]

DOUGLAS DC-3 DAKOTA

BELOW This remarkable executive-configured DC-3 has served Goodyear in Canada for 35 continuous years. Hangared all her life, she flies up to 14 board members out of Toronto. [*Stephen Piercey*]

BOTTOM Faded paintwork reveals that this time-worn DC-3 was once on the FAA's navaid checking fleet, its seal replaced by the 'logo' of Winky's Fish – The Flying Circus of Alaska.

RIGHT Fairbanks-Metro Field-based Air North maintained this 1938 DC-3A-197B in executive configuration, with contemporary interior furnishings. NC 18944 was built at Santa Monica and delivered to United in April 1938 as *Mainliner Omaha*, later *Mainliner Bend*. It logged 50,846 hours before retiring from United service in May 1954.

CENTER RIGHT Air North painted each of its DC-3s in a different livery. N3FY, in a mostly natural metal scheme reminiscent of the type's airline heyday in the US, bears the appropriate title *Grand Old Lady* and a nice line in grandma artwork.

BOTTOM RIGHT Pictured at Fairbanks-Metro Airport in July 1983, Air North DC-3 N8042X has since been sold to another Alaskan carrier, Audi Air. [*Photographs by Karl-Heinz Morawietz/Jörg Weier*]

DOUGLAS DC-3 DAKOTA

Plinth-mounted DC-3 CF-CPY in Canadian Pacific
livery is the star attraction at Whitehorse Airport in
the Yukon Territory. [*Stephen Piercey*]

LEFT ET-AGT, a C-47A delivered to the RAF as KG744 in 1944, seen at Ethiopia's newest airport of Bahar Dar on a charter passenger flight from Addis Ababa. Bahar Dar, located 385 miles north of Addis on the southern tip of Lake Tana, is being developed as a possible tourist center. [*David Oliver*]

CENTER LEFT One of Ethiopian Airlines' fleet of eight Dakotas, ET-AIB, starts up at Addis Ababa in January 1988. Built in 1946, this ex-Comm Airways DC-3D flies a scheduled passenger service to Dire Dawa, 220 miles to the east of the capital. [*David Oliver*]

ABOVE Undergoing a 200-hour check at the company's main base at Addis Ababa in January 1988 is Ethiopian Airlines' oldest Dakota – ET-AHQ. Built as a C-47 for the USAAF in August 1942, it served with the Yemen Arab Republic Air Force prior to joining Ethiopian in 1981. [*David Oliver*]

LEFT Ethiopian Airlines' Dakota freighter ET-AHG parked at Gondar, where the airstrip runs straight into the main street of the town. Another ex-RAF C-47A (KG794), 'AHG was bought from AD Aviation in 1979 and currently flies cargo between Gondar and Humera in Eritrea. [*David Oliver*]

DOUGLAS DC-3 DAKOTA

BELOW Ethiopian Airlines' Dakota ET-AGT parked at Gondar overlooking the Central Highlands. Situated 450 miles north of Addis Ababa and almost 8000 feet above sea level, the walled town of Gondar was Ethiopia's ancient capital. The 46-year-old C-47A is normally used for carrying freight to Goba, but can be fitted with canvas bench seats for 26 passengers. [*David Oliver*]

BELOW, INSET The view from ET-AGT as it flies over the country's Central Highlands, which can rise to 14,000 feet. The unpressurized DC-3 cruised at 11,000 feet during a 90-minute flight between Addis Ababa and Bahar Dar. [*David Oliver*]

DOUGLAS DC-3 DAKOTA

BELOW Dakota promota: Air Atlantique is Britain's last commercial DC-3 operator, and its flexible fleet of cargo and passenger aircraft are frequent sights at many European airports and beyond. Pictured here is G-AMPO, operating a flight over Welsh countryside. Retaining the colors of previous owner Eastern Airways, the Dak has since been repainted in Atlantique's dramatic livery. [*Stephen Piercey*]

RIGHT Television star: owned and operated by the Aces High film facilities group, this Douglas C-47 Dakota was rescued from a military fire dump, and has since become famous as the star in the series *Airline*. Masquerading as 'G-AGHY' of Ruskin Air Services, Dakota G-DAKS is photographed performing over her Duxford, Cambridgeshire base. [*Stephen Piercey*]

BELOW RIGHT Formerly G-AKNB, EI-BDU left the UK for the Emerald Isle in 1978 to fly with Dublin-based Clyden Airways. Here the Dakota undergoes engine checks on one of the wartime dispersals on the north side of Exeter Airport before delivery. [*Austin J. Brown/Mark R. Wagner*]

DOUGLAS DC-3 DAKOTA

Dakota G-AMPZ is owned by Exeter-based Harvest
Air and works in an anti-pollution role under a British
government contract.
[*Austin J. Brown/Mark R. Wagner*]

ABOVE Just like old times as Air Atlantique's DC-3 appears out of the mist on left base above the line-up at Eindhoven, Netherlands. Front to back we have the Flygande Veteraner DC-3 SE-CFP, Confederate Air Force R4D N151ZE, Air Luton G-AMPO, Dutch Dakota Association PH-DDA and Hibernian Dakota Flight N4565L.
[*Austin J. Brown/Mark R. Wagner*]

118

LEFT Happy Birthday! Fifty years young and still going strong. Complete with commemorative markings, Air Atlantique's Dakota 4 G-AMSV warms up its two 1200 hp Pratt & Whitney R-1830 Twin Wasps prior to the six-ship flypast at Eindhoven. [*Austin J. Brown/Mark R. Wagner*]

RIGHT G-AMSV flanks the Swedish Veteran's DC-3 prior to the action.
[*Austin J. Brown/Mark R. Wagner*]

BELOW Reputedly the only surviving Navy R4D-6, N151ZE *Ready 4 Duty* flies the Confederate and Union flags from the cockpit roof escape hatch. Bet the skipper's arms get tired.
[*Austin J. Brown/Mark R. Wagner*]

DOUGLAS DC-4

Fly-by by DC-4 fire-bomber No 18 of Aero Union, with civil registration N4218S. Several of the DC-4s had actually been C-54s and VC-54s of the Air Force, some seeing service on the Berlin Airlift in 1948–49. While a good pilot can always put the retardant down directly on the fire itself, in four missions out of five the task is instead to lay an impenetrable trail of retardant in the fire's path. The only drawback to using such aircraft is that they have to come back for a reload, and this takes time, needs a hustling ground crew and strains the aircraft in the landing and take-off. [*Philip Wallick*]

DOUGLAS DC-4

BELOW Gear up and an Aero Union DC-4 gets away from Chester, California. Note the crosswind, which has carried the aircraft well away from the runway centerline despite crabbing the machine round into the wind. This would have posed real problems with a B-17 and several other 'bombers'. [*Philip Wallick*]

BOTTOM Operating on this occasion out of Chico, California, a DC-4 of Aero Union banks steeply over the fire before letting go its 2000-gallon load over the best spot. [*Philip Wallick*]

BELOW The Douglas Commercials have been among the happier fire-bomber conversions, though these have tended to cost rather more initially than surplus bombers. Here, in fully operational trim, Aero Union DC-4 No 2 gets away from Chester. [*Philip Wallick*]

DOUGLAS DC-4

BELOW Take-off by a DC-4 from Chester on the power of its 1350-hp R-2000 engines, a slightly enlarged version of the familiar Pratt & Whitney Twin Wasp. Even at this point the pilot could still see the photographer, through the big and flat front windshield. [*Philip Wallick*]

BOTTOM Another Aero Union DC-4 comes in to land. As might be expected these aircraft posed no significant problems in performance or handling. [*Philip Wallick*]

BELOW Aero Union's Tanker 16 is a DC-4 which was painted in bicentennial livery for the 1976 celebrations at Chester. It was photographed still in the proud livery seven years later – during the rainy season, when its services would not be required. [*Philip Wallick*]

BOTTOM Until 1980, Eldorado Aviation employed a couple of DC-4s to supply cargo and company employees to uranium mines in Saskatchewan and other locations on northern Canada. This example is being loaded at Edmonton before making a night-time departure to Uranium City. [*Stephen Piercey*]

LEFT A timeless view across the Frigorificos Reyes freight ramp at La Paz, Bolivia. The B-17 from which the photo was taken had just returned from a meat farm in the province of Beni, while the DC-4 was preparing to leave on its round to San Borja and Santa Ana. The long-disused control tower, in the background, was full of old and dust-layered radio equipment. [*Stephen Piercey*]

RIGHT Crying out for mechanical (and cosmetic) attention, a hard-working Douglas DC-4 of Frigorificos Reyes arrives back at its La Paz base on three engines. Off-loaded and reloaded within a couple of hours, CP-1207 was airborne again en route to another meat farm in the Bolivian hinterland. [*Stephen Piercey*]

BELOW Frigorificos Reyes' DC-4 CP-1207 sits it out at La Paz. The aircraft is one of five owned by the company, but rarely are they all in service at one time. [*Stephen Piercey*]

LEFT Ready to roll: a Frigorificos Reyes DC-4, CP-1653, waits for take-off clearance at La Paz, Bolivia, before departing for Rurrenabaque, 160 miles to the north along the River Beni.

BELOW LEFT AND BELOW The same airplane off-loading supplies at Rurrenabaque after an uneventful landing on the grass field.

RIGHT Once the sexiest shape on the ramp, this DC-4 now brightens the backlot at La Paz. [*Photographs by Stephen Piercey*]

BELOW SATENA DC-4 FAC691 on the ramp at Bogota in May 1984 before departing on a flight to Puerto Asis in southern Colombia, via Neiva and Florencia. SATENA (*Servicio Aeronavegación a Territorios Nacionales*) is operated by the Colombian Air Force at the behest of the government to provide a lifeline for remote communities – a commercially untenable task for non-subsidized private airlines.

LEFT AND RIGHT En route: the flight deck of FAC691 is the vantage point as the Andes rise into view.

BELOW LEFT FAC1106 was destroyed in December 1979 when she flew into high ground while on a flight from Arauca to Cucuta, Colombia, claiming 21 lives. Replacement DC-4s are drafted from the air force inventory as required.
[*Photographs by Stephen Piercey*]

BELOW AND RIGHT DC-4 N67029 stripped back to bear metal during restoration work at San Jose, California, in September 1983. [*Stephen Piercey*]

BOTTOM All cowlings off Pacific Star Seafood Company Inc's C-54 Skymaster N898AL as ground crew prepare her 1540-hp Pratt & Whitney R-2800s for the 1983 fishing season. [*Karl-Heinz Morawietz/Jörg Weier*]

DOUGLAS DC-4

BELOW AND RIGHT Decidedly static Douglas DC-4
N74183 at Fort Lauderdale, minus No 3 engine. Built
in 1944 for the USAAF, it flew on the Hungarian
Airlift with Flying Tiger in 1956 and accumulated
58,615 hours before it was retired by Pacific
Western in 1972. [*Austin J. Brown/Mark R. Wagner*]

BELOW RIGHT One of Conifair's four DC-4s
(C-GXKN), pictured just after a smart respray at
Saint Jean Airport. [*Stephen Piercey*]

LEFT The last mission for the National Research Council's Canadair North Star, CF-SVP-X, was a week-long aerial survey trip across the Canadian Arctic in April 1976 under the callsign 'Research 8'. A magnetometer was housed in a 25-foot tail boom, visible here in a view of the aeroplane taking off from Resolute Bay, North-West Territories. Such was the stillness, the DC-4 was still audible 15 minutes later. [*Stephen Piercey*]

RIGHT Steep rock formations on Devon Island form a backdrop to the singing Merlins during a 1000-foot survey near Powell Inlet. When the North Star returned to her Ottawa base at the end of the week she had only ten engine hours remaining. [*Stephen Piercey*]

BELOW The Merlins performed well in temperatures of minus 30° or below. Retired and auctioned to a Texan dealer, this last flyable example was later impounded in one of the Bahamas islands. [*Stephen Piercey*]

DOUGLAS DC-4

BELOW Large numbers of surplus military Douglas C-54s have found a ready market in the United States as sprayers or borate bombers. Biegert Aviation's fleet of Chandler, Arizona-based sprayers were seen from a low-flying Cessna, patiently awaiting the start of a new season. [*Stephen Piercey*]

BOTTOM Rescued from the boneyard at Tucson, Arizona, this C-54 has been restored to pristine condition. The assorted junk in the background almost certainly won't be so lucky. [*Stephen Piercey*]

BELOW C-54 '117' warms its natural metal finish in the strong Arizona sunshine. [*Stephen Piercey*]

BOTTOM A good pre-owned C-54 can be bought for under $100,000 from the Aerospace Maintenance and Regeneration Center (formerly MASDC) at Davis

Monthan AFB, Arizona. Aero Union Corporation are the experts when it comes to converting old airliners into borate bombers or budworm sprayers to Standard Transport Category standard. A ventral pannier is the biggest modification, as on N963581/'160'. [*Stephen Piercey*]

BELOW Aviation Traders Limited of southern England engineered the unlovely but practical ATL-98 Carvair conversion of the Douglas DC-4 in 1961. The bulbous nose section with a raised flight deck enabled cars to be driven aboard through its hydraulically operated, sideways-opening nose door. [*Karl Heinz Morawietz/Jörg Weier*]

BELOW AND BOTTOM The Carvair also incorporated DC-6 brakes and the DC-7's larger fin and rudder to compensate for the additional keel area up front. This example, formerly British Air Ferries' *Porky Pete*, arrived in the USA in 1979 but made only a few flights into Alaska during 1982 while operated by the now defunct Gifford Aviation.
[*Karl-Heinz Morawietz/Jörg Weier*]

DOUGLAS DC-6

Colombia has always been a haven for old piston-engined aircraft. Conscious of poor safety records, its government wishes to abolish reciprocating airliners from its skies within a few years. Lineas Aereas del Caribe (LAC) of northern Colombia flies an immaculate fleet of Douglas DC-6As, although it has lost a number in fatal accidents. LAC is proud of its newly acquired DC-8 jets, and is phasing out its DC-6s. Seen taxying from Miami's northwest cargo area with 30,000 lb of industrial machinery, DC-6 HK-1707, in its 51,038th hour, flew into a mountain near Chiquinquira, north of Bogota, while on a flight from Trinidad to the Colombian capital in December 1978. [*Stephen Piercey*]

DOUGLAS DC-6

BELOW Routine three-engined arrival: number two engine feathered, this DC-6B of Transportes Aereos Mercantiles Panamericanos (TAMPA) arrives at its Medellin base in central Colombia. [*Stephen Piercey*]

BOTTOM Frigorificos Reyes' DC-6 CP-1650 pictured among the mountains at Rurrenabaque, Bolivia, after disgorging a respectable tally of fuel drums. [*Stephen Piercey*]

BELOW Thundering across Miami International Airport, Cayman Airways' DC-6B N61267 was lease-purchased from Rich International. Operating regular runs from Grand Cayman island, she was later repossessed for non-payment. [*Stephen Piercey*]

BOTTOM Just relieved of its cargo of fruit and vegetables from the Dominican Republic, Dominicana DC-6B HI-92 takes time out before reloading for the return trip. The teeming masses of Puerto Rico are the market for the growers of Santo Domingo. [*Austin J. Brown/Mark R. Wagner*]

DOUGLAS DC-6

BELOW A new machine for Aerovias, registered TG-CGO, this DC-6 prepares for loading before its return journey to Guatemala City. The carrier principally operates a fleet of Piper twins and Handley Page Heralds. [*Austin J. Brown/Mark R. Wagner*]

RIGHT It's alleged that this ex-Vortex DC-6, registered N33VX and possibly owned by Universal Air Leasing, is operated by what insiders know as the 'Contra Air Force', which is rumored to have been involved in the air dropping of military equipment for the Contra rebels in Nicaragua. To avoid the very real threat of being shot down by the Sandinistas, the drops are thought to have been carried out over Swan Island off the Honduran coast. [*Austin J. Brown/Mark R. Wagner*]

ABOVE Aerolineas El Salvador, SA de CV (known as AESA to the boys), operate this Douglas DC-6BF alongside one other out of San Salvador. YS-O5C is seen here at MIA undergoing major maintenance on number one, the prop having been removed. [*Austin J. Brown/Mark R. Wagner*]

RIGHT Douglas DC-6, N843TA, at Opa Locka a few weeks before it was due to make a delivery flight to Honduras along with HR-AKW, another Six said to belong to Pan Aviation. [*Austin J. Brown/Mark R. Wagner*]

Transporte Aereo Dominicano SA (TRADO)
appeared during 1980 operating a L-749
Constellation. Today the company owns two DC-6s,
one of which is withdrawn from use. HI-454 did not
move for over a month from its position on the Butler
Aviation ramp at MIA; surprisingly it is supposed to
be the active member of the fleet.
[*Austin J. Brown/Mark R. Wagner*]

DOUGLAS DC-6

BELOW Seagreen Air Transport of Antigua leased this
ex-Navy Douglas VC-118B from Paterson Aircraft to
supplement their two DC-3s, a DC-6, a DC-7 and a
Convair 880. [*Austin J. Brown/Mark R. Wagner*]

ABOVE With a somewhat suspicious overall olive
green paint scheme, this anonymous DC-6 had been
impounded at Santo Domingo early in 1980, though
airport officials would not comment on the reason for
her being laid up on the far side of the airfield. Similar
liveries on other aircraft have proved to be
advantageous while flying to small strips in South
America. [*Stephen Piercey*]

ABOVE A supposedly anonymous DC-6 rolls into San Juan Isla Verde in 1981 – but the registration (N928L) identifies it as one of the Bellomy Lawson fleet out of Miami. [*Austin J. Brown/Mark R. Wagner*]

DOUGLAS DC-6

BELOW Climbing into the evening sun, APA's DC-6 retracts the gear as it climbs out against a backdrop of Continental Airlines jets at MIA's main terminal. Based in Santo Domingo, APA lease this aircraft from Bellomy Lawson and it spends most of its time operating out of Miami.
[*Austin J. Brown/Mark R. Wagner*]

RIGHT AND BELOW RIGHT After landing on 27 Right, DC-6BF N94BL turns off the runway towards the Customs & Immigration building on the north side of the airport. Bellomy Lawson paint the spinners of their fleet in yellow to identify their aircraft from those of other DC-6 operators.
[*Austin J. Brown/Mark R. Wagner*]

LEFT Looking very smart and business-like, Trans-Air-Link's DC-6 N872TA receives attention to its nose wheel oleo at Miami.

BELOW LEFT TAL's N841TA pictured at home base after a trip to St Thomas in the US Virgin Islands.

RIGHT A bare metal TAL DC-6AC and a white TAL DC-6A on the company ramp at Miami.

BELOW Well tucked away behind N872TA in a quiet corner of the TAL ramp was this Convair 440, N910RC, due to come on line as the baby of the fleet.

BOTTOM TAL's DC-6 N841TA gets off smartly at St Thomas to clear the hill at the upwind end of Runway One Zero en route back to Miami via San Juan. [*Photographs by Austin J. Brown/Mark R. Wagner*]

BELOW AND BELOW RIGHT The water container is entirely external to the pressurized fuselage, being slung beneath in a way that avoids the tank having to carry any inflight loads other than the evenly distributed mass of water. Internal baffles cut down

BELOW This DC-6 is one of the more stylishly painted firefighting tankers. Operating from Chico, California, it serves along with a fleet of other types including the Neptune parked to the rear. These great Douglases have paddle-blade propellers turned by 2500-horsepower Double Wasps, which make light work of a 3000-gallon load. The anti-dazzle black panel is found on virtually all water bombers to make it easier to look ahead over the nose in brilliant sunshine. The pointed nose shows that radar was fitted, and this – usually unlike the pressurization system – is invariably maintained in operative condition. [*Philip Wallick*]

sloshing. On pilot command the entire load can be dumped by opening flaps along each side over the full length; this avoids any change in longitudinal trim as the water leaves, which at low level could be dangerous. [*Philip Wallick*]

BELOW Ground checkout of the retardant installation in a firefighting DC-6, using plain water. The belly tank added to these aircraft water. The belly tank added to these aircraft usually has a capacity of 3000 US gallons, but this example belongs to the Sécurité Civile in France and is calibrated in litres. A 3000 US gallon load, ignoring the tank and installation, represents a dead weight of 25,000 lb. [*David Oliver*]

DOUGLAS DC-6

RIGHT The majority of active DC-6s are found in North, South and Central America. Under Colombian ownership, this DC-6 was seized in Kansas during 1977 after landing on a highway in the middle of the night with a large consignment of marijuana. Today she is Miami-based as N6584C. [*Stephen Piercey*]

BELOW The classic lines of the big 'Dougs' are evident in this full frontal of Rich International's N61267. She awaited her crew for a flight to the Cayman Islands, but the lack of a Cuban overfly permit resulted in a delayed departure. [*Stephen Piercey*]

CENTER RIGHT Powered by R-2800 Double Wasp engines and with a pressurized fuselage, the DC-6 was instantly distinguishable from the wartime DC-4 by its square passenger windows. Here an American Airlines DC-6 still wears its old livery whilst waiting for conversion to its new role as a fire-bomber. [*Philip Wallick*]

BOTTOM RIGHT Under normal circumstances Conair would be a somewhat suspicious name for an aircraft operator, but in this case it refers to the airborne protection of Canada's rich coniferous forests. This is borate DC-6, C-GIOY/'48'. [*Stephen Piercey*]

DOUGLAS DC-6

BELOW During 1978 more than 30 DC-6s were flying out of Willow Run Airport, Detroit, in support of the three giant US car manufacturers – Ford, General Motors and Chrysler. The recession affected this industry badly, leaving several large fleets without work. Trans Continental Airlines survived, but its once large fleet has been reduced to a couple of aircraft. [*Stephen Piercey*]

RIGHT Though neither an air force nor an airline, France's Sécurité Civile is proud of its triangle-in-circle insignia. Here it adorns a beautifully prepared DC-6B, seen at Marseilles Marignane. [*David Oliver*]

CENTER RIGHT This DC-6B of the Sécurité Civile has a different tank installation, similar to that on the DC-6B at Chico (see page 156). [*David Oliver*]

ABOVE N12347, one of NPT's DC-6As, was built at Santa Monica in 1953 for the Flying Tiger Line. Leased to Northwest Airlines until 1961, she subsequently flew with Zantop, Southern Airways and TAISA of Costa Rica before returning to the USA in 1975 for service as a fire-bomber with Sis-Q Flying Services in California. The versatile Six made the 'Last Frontier' state her home in 1980. [*Karl-Heinz Morawietz/Jörg Weier*]

RIGHT Finnish carrier Kar-Air's spotless swing-tail DC-6B OH-KDA was one of two aircraft so converted by SABENA at Brussels in 1968. She operated the Helsinki-London cargo schedule for Finnair in the early 1980s, until replaced by a DC-9. Photographed at Manchester shortly before operating one of the last trips from England, OH-KDA was sold during 1982 and now flies for a Florida operator. [*Stephen Piercey*]

160

DOUGLAS DC-6

BELOW The Jaguar XK in the foreground comes a poor second to this towering DC-6 of Air Atlantique. Freight doors open, the pristine 'X-ray Charlie' has an aura of understated efficiency. Built as a 'Pax' configuration DC-6B model, she made her maiden flight on 22 September 1958 and was delivered to Civil Air Transport, China, six days later, and went on to serve with CAAC before being transferred to Royal Air Lao in August 1968. After five years of operations with Air America and Air Asia, the aircraft was converted to 'A' status in Taiwan, and fitted with a strengthened floor and freight doors. Sold to Southern Air Transport of Miami in September 1973, she was acquired by Rosenberg Aviation Inc in June 1976 before joining Trans Continental in April 1978. When this picture was taken at Coventry, England (June 1987), G-SIXC had flown around 35,800 hours. [*Austin J. Brown/Mark R. Wagner*]

BELOW Air Atlantique's DC-6 received its UK Certificate of Airworthiness on 7 April 1987 and began revenue-earning flights shortly afterwards. The aircraft was bought from Trans Continental Airlines and the 'Big Six' arrived at Coventry on 22 March 1987 after a 14 hr 20 min ferry flight from Gander, Newfoundland, having prepositioned there from Willow Run Airport in Detroit, Michigan, the previous day. [*Austin J. Brown/Mark R. Wagner*]

ABOVE Everything's looking good, so let's start No 1. OK, crack the throttle, squeeze the starter switches, wait for one-two-three-four-five-six blades, switch ignition to 'both' and depress the primer switch . . . there, she's caught. That big round R-2800 really is a wonderful engine. Stabilize at 800 rpm using primer fuel, then carefully increase the mixture as you're backing off on the primer. Nothing to it for DC-6 N43872 at Saarbrücken in May 1982. [*Austin J. Brown/Mark R. Wagner*]

ABOVE Northern Air Cargo flies scheduled services to 23 communities within Alaska, keeping the reliable 'Dizzy Sixes' active 24 hours a day. As soon as the last piece of cargo is secured and N313RS has taken on a load of 100 octane, she's off the blocks and bound for Kodiak Island, an hour and a half's flying time away.

LEFT Ground power carts are close companions of the aircraft on Northern Air Cargo's ramp.

ABOVE RIGHT Upward opening fore and aft freight doors were a standard feature of the DC-6A, whose reinforced cabin floor can take up to 28,188 lbs of cargo.

RIGHT NAC boasts the world's biggest fleet of DC-6s, and the aircraft may even rival Maytags for dependability and long service.
[*Photographs by Karl-Heinz Morawietz/Jörg Weier*]

LEFT Cargo netted, paperwork complete and doors secured, NAC's Captain Doug Lee fires up Eighty Bravo's 10,000 horses as she prepares to depart from Anchorage.

BELOW LEFT Fortunately the NAC fleet has a better accident record than this Chevrolet truck.

BELOW The virginal white DC-6A N7780B was built for cargo carrier Riddle, but was once owned by multi-millionaire recluse Howard Hughes, perhaps accounting for its incredibly low total of only 9 hr 50 min logged when NAC bought it in 1973.

[Photographs by Karl-Heinz Morawietz/Jörg Weier]

ABOVE LEFT AND ABOVE Stage struck. This beautiful nose art was painted on N99330's aluminum canvas by a talented young lady from Tucson, but sadly not retained when the travel weary DC-6A/C went into service with Northern Air Cargo. The aircraft was bought from Carnegie Holdings of Edmonton, Canada in 1987 and has been around a bit, as the flags of all nations attest.
[*Karl-Heinz Morawietz/Jörg Weier*]

LEFT Seen in snow and sunshine, N6813C was built for (but never delivered to) the British independent carrier Airwork. Her first operator was Slick Airways, and she became Northern Air Cargo's first DC-6A in 1969. One Three Charlie was christened *Taiwan Clipper* after crossing the Pacific to Taiwan for a major overhaul.
[*Karl-Heinz Morawietz/Jörg Weier*]

LEFT Three Six Fox's wingtip points to the 6509-foot summit of Black Peak Mountain. The aircraft is a former USAF C-118A acquired from the Military Aircraft Storage and Disposition Centre (MASDC) 'boneyard' at Davis-Monthan AFB, Arizona. [*Karl-Heinz Morawietz/Jörg Weier*]

BELOW LEFT Despite having seen more than 30 summers (and harsh winters), Northern Air Cargo's Douglases are in sparkling condition, as reflected by the polished skin of DC-6A N1377K. [*Karl-Heinz Morawietz/Jörg Weier*]

RIGHT Open air maintenance is SOP in the hectic short Alaskan summer to keep downtime to the minimum. Here a decowled 2500 hp Double Wasp CB17 of DC-6A N4206L gets a dose of tender loving care from an NAC powerplant expert. [*Karl-Heinz Morawietz/Jörg Weier*]

BELOW Big friend, slightly smaller friend: a Flying Tigers' Boeing 747-200F towers over Northern Air Cargo's bulk tanker on the cargo ramp. The all-freight Jumbo's cargo capacity is almost double the maximum take-off weight of a DC-6A – but don't try putting one into a short airstrip. [*Karl-Heinz Morawietz/Jörg Weier*]

DOUGLAS DC-7

RIGHT AND BELOW T & G Aviation of Chandler, Arizona, is probably the world's biggest operator of DC-7 borate bombers. This DC-7C, N5903, looks to be in superb condition. [*Stephen Piercey*]

BELOW Most powerful of all the piston-engined Douglas Commercials, the DC-7 still carries the same 3000 US gallon load as the DC-6. This example is doing a test drop with plain water at Chico in 1975. Over a fire it would probably get down to rather lower altitude if the terrain permitted. [*Philip Wallick*]

BELOW RIGHT Assisted by a ground power truck a DC-7 starts its 3250-hp Wright R-3350 Turbo-Compound engines, which though massive and expensive offered unprecedented power and fuel economy. The pilot may be checking flap operation; full landing flap has been selected. [*Philip Wallick*]

Top The essential stepladder is pulled on board a DC-7C of Aero Union. The ultimate piston-engined DC, the famed Seven Seas was a happy result of adding 5 feet to each wing center section. This gave more lift, made room for more fuel and moved the propellers away from the fuselage so that not even 3400-hp Turbo-Compounds caused quite such a racket and vibration inside the cabin. [*Philip Wallick*]

Above A DC-7C Seven Seas tanker about to taxi out. Douglas achieved such a pinnacle of aerodynamic refinement with the 7C that its drag was the same as that of a rod stretched between the wingtips with a diameter of one inch. [*Philip Wallick*]

Above About to reach *terra firma* from the lofty elevation of a Seven Seas. Costly to maintain and operate, the DC-7C was designed to fly the North Atlantic non-stop, and what's really needed is some way of putting its enormous internal fuel capacity to work with fire retardant instead of 115/145-grade gasoline. In firefighting a typical mission radius is more like 40 miles rather than 4000. [*Philip Wallick*]

Top A DC-7B that eagerly awaits the summer season of forest fires is T & G Aviation's 'borate bomber' N51701. Note the large tank slung underneath her belly. The cabin of the aircraft is empty. [*Stephen Piercey*]

Above DC-7B N4887C, a former Delta Air Lines flagship, flies on contract aerial firefighting missions from bases in the Western states. She was seen in Arizona being spruced up before a US Forestry Service inspection so that she could take part in the demanding 1981 fire season. [*Stephen Piercey*]

DOUGLAS DC-7

BELOW Halfway house: originally in scheduled service with an airline, this DC-7 was one of several operated by Ports of Call, a Denver charter company, before being converted as a fire-bomber in the 1970s. By chance, back in 1953 Douglas Aircraft was engaged in testing the prototype DC-7 and used water as ballast. When the load was dumped through a 6-inch pipe it was found it wetted the ground, and special tests took place at Arcadia and Palmdale. But in those days the $1,600,000 flagship was totally uneconomic as a firefighter; 20 years of depreciation did the trick, however. [*Philip Wallick*]

BOTTOM This old DC-7C hauled cargoes of fish, avocados, mangoes and fishing tackle to points in the Caribbean during the late 1970s. In more recent years she was grounded by the FAA with a staggering 120 airworthiness violations. [*Stephen Piercey*]

Below Seen loading at Kingston, Jamaica, Trans-Air-Link's N869TA started life in July 1957 when it was delivered to KLM as a DC-7C (PH-DSI). During August 1962 the DC-7C was converted to a CF freighter and eventually found its way into Biafra. By 1972 it was reported as being semi-derelict at Salisbury, Rhodesia. The next information indicates it was operated by Air Gabon Cargo (1978), Air Trans Africa (1979) then the Rhodesia-Zimbabwe Air Force (1980). During the early 1980s it was owned by Affretair (VP-YTY), after which it was ferried across to Florida and joined TAL during 1984.
[*Austin J. Brown/Mark R. Wagner*]

Bottom Fisheye view of the three-man team at the sharp end of the Seven approaching the north Cuban coastline at 9000 feet.
[*Austin J. Brown/Mark R. Wagner*]

179

LEFT At 2200 rpm and 32 inches of manifold pressure speed is 200 knots at a cruising altitude of 9000 feet.

BELOW LEFT There's not much about the DC-7 that TAL's maintenance inspector 'Pete' doesn't know. The four Wright R-3350 fuel-injected Turbo-Compound engines were originally rated at 3400 hp with the old 115/145 octane 'hot' fuel, but with current 100LL avgas only 2800 hp is produced.

RIGHT Jamaica Air Freighters unload at Kingston.

BELOW TAL's DC-7CF loads up with a variety of goods grossing 127,000 lb.
[*Photographs by Austin J. Brown/Mark R. Wagner*]

LEFT N16465 of La Mancha Aire fires up her massive Wright 3350s at Port of Spain, Trinidad. Her cargo? 36,000 lb of toilet rolls and biscuits destined for a Caribbean island. The Seven carries around 8000 lb more than a Six as well as cruising a little faster. [*Stephen Piercey*]

RIGHT LMA's DC-7 arrives in the picturesque island of St Kitts – and a 1931 Austin that has definitely seen better days offloads boxes of biscuits and cheese balls, the latter a Christmas delicacy on the island. [*Stephen Piercey*]

BELOW Florida's La Mancha Aire was formed to operate Douglas DC-7 freighters during 1979. Its first aircraft, a DC-7B, was rebuilt from scratch by the airline at a cost of $400,000. Illustrated here is its second aircraft (since sold), a former BOAC DC-7C. [*Stephen Piercey*]

BELOW RIGHT Trans-Air-Link's DC-7CF seen through the eye of a cowling. [*Austin J. Brown/Mark R. Wagner*]

LEFT The number of active DC-7s is rapidly dwindling. Photographed from the right-hand seat of a DC-7 camera ship in close formation is La Mancha Aire's N16465, performing near the Venezuelan coast in 1982. The previous evening she had flown horses down to Rochambeau in French Guiana. The aircraft is also featured on the previous two pages. [*Stephen Piercey*]

BELOW LEFT A 10,000 mile ferry flight across the African and South American continents was completed by this 26-year-old DC-7C in 1982, after she was bought by La Mancha Aire of Florida from Affretair, Zimbabwe. She is seen here at Recifé, Brazil, where fuel was uplifted. [*Stephen Piercey*]

BELOW During the long ferry flight from Harare, Zimbabwe, to Florida via the Ivory Coast (West Africa), Brazil, Surinam and Venezuela, La Mancha Aire paid more in fuel costs than it did for the aeroplane. Still retaining Affretair colors, VP-YTY basked in Abidjan sunshine, ready to cross the South Atlantic Ocean to Brazil on the second leg of the trip. [*Stephen Piercey*]

Left The Wright stuff: the 7C is powered by four 3400 hp TC18 Turbo-Compound (R-3350-EA1) 18-cylinder two-row radials housed in titanium nacelles. N90802's port inner needs a spinner. In its heyday the DC-7C was a peerless performer. Thanks to its quintessential aerodynamics and abundant power, the 'Seven Seas' could carry over 100 cosseted passengers non-stop across the North Atlantic (the first aircraft to do so) at 345 mph, even against the strength-sapping jetstreams encountered on the westerly route. [*Stephen Piercey*]

Above The 7C was the ultimate development of the magnificent 'Seven', which was also the first airliner to fly non-stop from coast to coast across the United States, a feat it achieved in November 1953. Almost 30 years after it rolled off the production line at Santa Monica, N90802 sports a ventral borate tank with a capacity of 3000 US gallons (27,375 lb). [*Stephen Piercey*]

Right A regal DC-7C, N74303 was delivered to Pan Am in July 1956 as *Clipper Ocean Rover*. Acquired by Club International in 1972, the aircraft still looked pretty smart in the maintenance area at Miami International seven years later. [*Austin J. Brown/Mark R. Wagner*]

BELOW Douglas dominated the market for four-engined transports, building a total of 2284. The company built the last of 121 DC-7Cs in 1958; Arizona is probably home for most of the handful which survive. [*Stephen Piercey*]

LEFT Old BOAC DC-7C still going strong as N9000T of Seagreen Air Transport. Registered in Antigua but officially based in Miami, '9000T takes on a cargo of eggs for Kingston, Jamaica. [*Stephen Piercey*]

BELOW LEFT DC-7B N4889C still has her full complement of Turbo-Compounds, but who needs a thirsty 'Seven' without a strengthened cargo floor?

Incidentally, the extended wing center section added to the 7C lengthened the span by 10 ft (to 127 ft 6 in) and pushed the engines further outboard – a feature which reduced drag and set a new low in cabin noise and vibration. [*Stephen Piercey*]

BELOW Glory daze: two DC-7Bs that have enjoyed better times stare into oblivion. [*Stephen Piercey*]

FAIRCHILD C-119 Flying Boxcar

RIGHT Stebbins & Ambler's fleet comprises just one aircraft, this Fairchild C-119, with two other grounded Boxcars cannibalized for spares to keep N1394N Flying.

BELOW A perfect example of self-help, 'Alaska's first native air transport company' was formed by the villages of Stebbins and Ambler to keep themselves supplied with vital goods.

[Photographs by Karl-Heinz Morawietz/Jörg Weier]

TOP AND TOP RIGHT N1394N's 3500 hp Wright R-3500s are run up under critical eyes prior to the start of a trip over the high peaks of the Chigmit mountain range to Manokotak, 300 miles south-east of Anchorage on Nushagak Bay. Stebbins & Ambler are restricted to VFR operations, so destination and alternate airports and en route weather must be within VMC limits.

ABOVE Shot from the navigator's astrodome and neatly framed by VHF antennae is the C-119's dorsally-mounted Stewart-Davis jet booster pack – a podded 3800 lb st Westinghouse J34 turbojet engine which provides enhanced take-off and climb performance and greater safety margins when operating from short runways in mountainous terrain.

RIGHT There's only one flight crew, made up of pilot Jim Devine, copilot Bob Jaidinger and engineer John Reffett, so it's a case of 'all hands to the pump' when topping off N1394N's fuel tanks. After years of bad weather the Boxcar's wing leading edges look like they've been attacked with a ball-peen hammer. [*Photographs by Karl-Heinz Morawietz/Jörg Weier*]

LEFT Perfect VFR weather and an eye-level view of Alaska's spectacular landscape make for a memorable trip over the Chigmits.

BELOW LEFT Climbing fast is not the Boxcar's forte. As flight engineer John Reffett put it, 'Before we reach 12,000 feet we're in Japan.'

BELOW After a two-hour flight the Stebbins & Ambler crew arrive at Manokotak's narrow, 2600-foot gravel airstrip: uncluttered airspace, little traffic and no sign of noise abatement procedures or protesting environmentalists.

[*Photographs by Karl-Heinz Morawietz/Jörg Weier*]

BELOW With maximum reverse thrust the C-119 came to a halt within feet of the strip's end. Harsh reverse pitch caused three litres of hydraulic fluid to escape through the propeller's dome seals.

LEFT When the crew had replenished vital fluids they faced the additional chore of unloading the Boxcar with no outside help save for a pair of C-119 buffs/photographers.

RIGHT 'Ready to rock'n'roll!' calls Captain Jim Devine – and copilot Bob Jaidinger hangs onto a windscreen brace as the C-119, Wrights turning and J34 burning, starts its take-off run down Manokotak's testing strip.
[*Photographs by Karl-Heinz Morawietz/Jörg Weier*]

FAIRCHILD C-119 FLYING BOXCAR

BELOW C-119 N8504X gets attention from Northern Pacific Transport maintenance staff at NPT's Anchorage base. The Flying Boxcar first flew in 1947 and was built by Fairchild and Kaiser Industries, remaining in production until October 1955, when the 112th aircraft was delivered to the USAF.

BOTTOM Founded by Gerald C. Ball, Northern Pacific Transport is one of the longest established cargo carriers in Alaska. It operates a mixed fleet of mostly MASDC-surplus Douglas C-47s, C-118s and Fairchild C-82 Pockets and C-119 Boxcars, hauling general cargo and fish.

BELOW Looking for oil leaks is par for the course when your aeroplanes fly on big round engines, and a thorough ground check of the Boxcar's 3500 hp Wright R-3350-89 Cyclone engines is vital before return to service. Never blessed with excess performance at high gross weights, the aircraft is unflatteringly known as the 'flying coffin' among Boxcar old-timers. This one has a podded Westinghouse J34 jet engine to boost take-off and climb performance – a common add-on to commercially operated C-119s.
[*Photographs by Karl-Heinz Morawietz/Jörg Weier*]

LEFT This beautifully painted C-119 fire-bomber has the Steward-Davis jet booster pack on top, housing a Westinghouse J34. [*Philip Wallick*]

BELOW LEFT A C-119 of Aero Union's great fleet thunders out of Chico, California. With brilliant rate of roll and spring-tab elevators there was no problem in control (to an experienced pilot, who, for example, would avoid aileron stalls at even 170 knots), but on landing the ineffective flaps were rated as 'terrible'. [*Philip Wallick*]

BELOW There are only five C-119s present, but the tail booms tend to multiply the numbers. With the jet booster these were not bad aircraft, but they suffered from one slight handicap: the wings tended to fall off. This slightly bothered the pilots, who eventually considered it might be preferable if they picked a different kind of tanker. In fairness to Fairchild, the original design never envisaged intensive flying with massive loads at ground level. Known also as the Dollar-nineteen, the Boxcar was regarded as surprisingly agile but underpowered. [*Philip Wallick*]

FAIRCHILD C-123 Provider

Aero Union's Provider No 63 awaits the steep approach of a fellow firefighting DC-4 after a summer mission out of Chico. The scene looks beautiful, but it's to preserve such scenery that the tankers fly their hazardous missions. The C-123 was one of the tankers whose retardant installation ended in flush belly doors; when the load of red-dyed liquid gushed forth it stained the belly all the way back to the tip of the tailcone. [*Philip Wallick*]

Above Originally developed by Chase Aircraft during the Korean War, the C-123 was in the class of the C-119 and had similar R-2800 engines, but in general it was lighter and more efficient. It was especially good as the C-123K with underwing jet booster pods (General Electric J85s of 2850 lb thrust each, as fitted here), which made it almost sprightly.
[*Philip Wallick*]

Right The one that never made it out – its partner in crime never made it back. Provider N681DG was said to have left the Davis Monthan boneyard as one of a pair. The other aircraft was allegedly N4410F, the one shot down by the Sandinistas north of San Carlos in Nicaragua in 1986 as it attempted to drop small arms and uniforms to the Contras. In the aftermath of this embarrassing incident, the *Miami Herald* newspaper apparently published a picture which clearly showed an Air America operations manual lying in the wreckage. [*Austin J. Brown/Mark R. Wagner*]

FAIRCHILD C-123 PROVIDER

This anonymous but immaculate Fairchild C-123 Provider was spotted on the perimeter at Opa Locka. The head-on shot of the same aircraft illustrates the 'wide body' design which made the type such a useful workhorse. [*Austin J. Brown/Mark R. Wagner*]

LOCKHEED
Constellation

Spray bars with 68 nozzles each side are attached to the wing trailing edge of this Conifair Constellation. Inside the fuselage are two large tanks which hold about 3000 gallons of 'goop', a term used for the oil and chemical mixture with which they spray. The four to six-week spraying season in Quebec results in millions of acres of forrested land being treated against the villainous budworm. [*Stephen Piercey*]

RIGHT Constellation C-GXKR is one of a pair of lusty 749ers operated by Conifair Aviation Inc in northern Quebec. [*Stephen Piercey*]

ABOVE Goop is a cocktail of diesel fuel and malathion with a dash of red dye to aid visual monitoring. Although it's bad news for budworms, the spray is at worst a passing irritant to other forest creatures. [*Stephen Piercey*]

RIGHT Conifair started fighting the budworm in 1979 with a fleet of three Constellations. Today the spotless, ever-growing fleet consists of two Connies, four DC-4s and three DC-6s. [*Stephen Piercey*]

BELOW Calm conditions are required for a smooth, accurate application. When the going gets rough, the goop stops flowing. [*Stephen Piercey*]

BELOW A Conifair Connie's port pair in full cry at the start of a spraying run. [*Stephen Piercey*]

BELOW The dawn silence of a peaceful town in Quebec is shattered as Conifair Aviation's Constellation C-GXKO claws skywards for an early morning spraying sortie in June 1981. [*Stephen Piercey*]

RIGHT Ideal spraying time for the 'budworm bombers' is when the air is most still, early morning or evening. Captured from an Aztec chase plane, one of the Connies is seen in action one evening in the region of Matane, Quebec. Its chemical 'cargo' is colored to aid visual monitoring. [*Stephen Piercey*]

LOCKHEED CONSTELLATION

BELOW There's good reason for this Super Constellation to fly with her overwing emergency exits removed: it was an attempt to reduce the intense heat in the cabin given off by terrified livestock. On the Connie's empty return sectors it was intended to reduce the aroma of a six-inch layer of dung deposited on the cabin floor by the outward-bound cargo! The aircraft, N1007C, is pictured on finals to Miami in September 1977. [*Stephen Piercey*]

RIGHT The beautiful old Constellation N6021C flew from Miami for many years with Mack McKendree's Unlimited Leasing, Inc. Sold in 1979, the 749 was seized in northern Florida with a 36,000 lb cargo of marijuana. After five years in open storage the Connie was flown away by a brave Dominican aircrew in August 1983 for a new life in the Caribbean. [*Stephen Piercey*]

RIGHT Constellation 749 N6021C nears the Miami Beach area on long finals to Miami. Barely months after this shot was taken the old Connie was on finals to some dirt strip in northern Colombia to collect a multi-million dollar cargo of marijuana. She was one that did not get away, being seized in Panama City, Florida. [*Stephen Piercey*]

LEFT Many 'reciprocating' aircrew are proud to be flying the last of the piston giants – but others are not so prop-proud. Such misguided individuals long for the day they can climb into a jet. [*Stephen Piercey*]

LEFT This 049 Connie was one of the oldest surviving in the 1970s. She always flew chock-a-block with Quisqueyana on the Santo Domingo-San Juan route, in direct competition with Dominicana de Aviacion (727) and Eastern Airlines (L-1011). Eventually the Dominican Republic Government pulled the carrier's license in January 1979 on the grounds that its fleet of two serviceable Constellations was unsafe. [*Stephen Piercey*]

LEFT Passenger-carrying Lockheed Constellations remained operational as late as January 1979. Aerovias Quisqueyana of the Dominican Republic was the final passenger operator anywhere and offered twice-daily, regularly overbooked services in its 80-seat 049 and 749 aircraft between Santo Domingo and San Juan. Early morning travelers were given a cup of rum instead of coffee. This 1946-vintage 049 was retired in 1977. It's remarkable that she was still taking passenger fares so late in life – and ironic that the last Constellations to carry passengers were the oldest in existence. [*Stephen Piercey*]

ABOVE A typically smokey start-up for a Super Constellation's Wright 3350. In later life, overhaul times for these temperamental engines averaged 1200 hours, although some operators were known to pass the 3000-hour mark. [*Stephen Piercey*]

BELOW Aerochago SA operated Super Constellation HI-228 into San Juan, Dominican Republic, in January 1982, where the aircraft's cargo was unloaded one box at a time. Southern Flyer's DC-3s lurk in the background, and a Casair C-46 waits on the stand. [*Austin J. Brown/Mark R. Wagner*]

RIGHT The very low morning light catches this Connie half-asleep on the ramp at San Juan. TRADO used 749A Constellation HI-332 to haul fruit and vegetables for a short while in 1980. [*Austin J. Brown/Mark R. Wagner*]

LOCKHEED CONSTELLATION

BELOW Aerotours operated two 1049C Super Connies through San Juan, Dominican Republic, in 1979–80, HI-329 being one of them. They were a rare sight indeed, even in the late 1970s, and once seen they were never forgotten. This Connie was built for Eastern Airlines and delivered in February 1954. It was converted to a freighter shortly after leaving Eastern, and even became a sprayer in 1974 before reverting to passenger operations. [*Austin J. Brown/Mark R. Wagner*]

ABOVE Early model 1049 HI-228 is the oldest flying Super Constellation. Based at Santo Domingo for many years with Aerotours Dominicano, she now flies with Aerochago SA of the same city under a lease agreement with Aerotours. Photographed uplifting produce in St Croix, HI-228 remains as the last commercially operated Connie anywhere – for the time being. [*Stephen Piercey*]

BELOW Former USAF Constellation 749 entered service with Aerolineas Argo of the Dominican Republic as HI-328 in 1979 following ten years as a Wyoming-based sprayer. She island-hopped in the Caribbean with fresh produce until one starlit night in October 1981 when her crew flew her into the sea off the coast of St Thomas. Argo replaced the wrecked Connie with a sistership – but this, too, was grounded after the company ceased trading early in 1983. [*Stephen Piercey*]

ABOVE Workhorse of the Caribbean for five years was the Air Cargo Support Super Constellation N1007C. Seen here uplifting produce at La Romana in the Dominican Republic, she was retired from service and flown to Opa Locka Airport for storage in February 1982. [*Stephen Piercey*]

LEFT After a patient three-year wait, *Propliner* scooped every other aviation magazine in 1984 when it carried a major feature on the Super Constellations operated by the Indian Air Force and Navy. Despite some corrosion problems in the belly area, the serviceable Air Force Connies were still in outstanding condition. Pictured at Lohegaon AFB, Pune, on 6 January 1984, BG583 (foreground) made its last flight the previous November; the airplane is currently held in storage pending a decision to fly her to the Air Force museum in New Delhi. Like the other eight Indian Connies, this 1049G was a hand-me-down from flag carrier Air India. BG579 (background) began her Air Force career in 1962 and served continuously with No 6 Squadron, transporting personnel and general cargo throughout the Indian subcontinent until she was withdrawn from service on 31 March 1984. During the course of his on-the-spot report, Stephen Piercey made a 28-minute flight aboard this aircraft from Pune to Santa Cruz – the highlight of an historic visit. [*Stephen Piercey*]

LEFT IN316 has never been the same since the landing gear was retracted accidentally as it taxied at Goa on 11 January 1983. Fortunately, the Indian Navy received a batch of Soviet Ilyushin Il-38s to replace the clapped-out Connies. The Indian Navy assumed responsibility for all maritime patrol duties in 1976, and five 1049s were duly transfered from the Air Force inventory to equip No 312 Squadron. All the aircraft were modified for their new role and featured a Thorn EMI ASV.21 multi-mode search radar mounted in a ventral 'dustbin' behind the nosewheel doors. [*Stephen Piercey*]

ABOVE California's Classic Air hoped to carry sightseers in its former US Air Force and Navy Super Constellations to the Grand Canyon and other tourist sites, but the airworthiness authorities reckoned differently. One aircraft (N1104W, in the foreground) had seats installed, taken from an El Al Boeing 747. [*Stephen Piercey*]

LOCKHEED CONSTELLATION

BELOW The world's last flyable 049 Connie, N90816, parked at Fort Lauderdale. She hadn't been in the air since arriving from California one stormy day in 1978.

BELOW RIGHT AND BOTTOM Super Constellation N73544 at Camarillo Airport near Burbank in January 1984 after an eventful ferry flight from Chino – a journey punctuated by an engine shutdown and numerous expletives from her crew. LA-based Classic Air purchased this ex-US Air Force C-121C after the Connie became surplus to spraying requirements. A stillborn attempt to refurbish the airplane for

passenger services, including a half-hearted attack with a spray gun, seems to have ended in stalemate.

RIGHT AND BOTTOM RIGHT Mighty Lockheed 1649 Starliner being prepared during 1983 for her first flight since 1976 for her new owner, Maine-born Maurice Roundy, a self-confessed Connie buff. During the late summer the 1649's engines were turning for the first time in seven years and in the November his gracious N7316C flew away from Stewart Airport, New York.
[*Photographs by Stephen Piercey*]

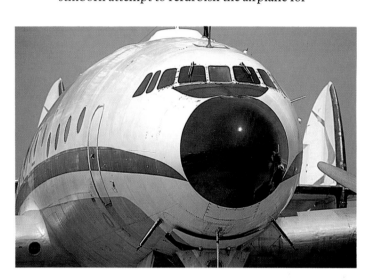

LOCKHEED
Neptune

LEFT Beautifully painted in Aero Union livery, P-2H Tanker 01 was still not fully converted when these photographs were taken, and (as the gap in the former weapon bay shows) the retardant tank had not then been fitted. The big and powerful P-2 can take a 3000-US gallon load. This one has a new metal nose. [*Philip Wallick*]

BELOW Though it was first flown as long ago as 1954, the final model of Neptune, at first called the P2V-7 and after 1962 the P-2H (or SP-2H in anti-submarine form), served in front-line Navy squadrons until 1966, and much longer with the Reserves. One of its features was this completely new cockpit, giving good all-round visibility. [*Philip Wallick*]

LOCKHEED NEPTUNE

BELOW The Lockheed P-2 Neptune is one of the biggest and most powerful of the twin-engined tankers. Indeed, some might be considered four-engined, because they have jet booster pods, but these are not fitted to this example. P-2s began to fight fires in 1969, and substantial numbers serve in Oregon. It will probably be many years before something with turbine engines can come along and do a better job. [*Philip Wallick*]

RIGHT Successor to the PV-2 Harpoon on the Lockheed production line, the Neptune was one of the first aircraft to be fitted with MAD (magnetic anomaly detection) gear, which finds submarines by detecting distortion caused to the Earth's magnetic field. The sensor had to be as far as possible from the disturbance caused by the aircraft itself, so it was put at the tip of a very long tail extension. It was left on Tanker 01, but many tanker P-2s had the tail cut short. [*Philip Wallick*]

BELOW RIGHT Main engines of the P-2H are two Wright R-3350-32W Turbo-Compounds, each rated at 3500 horsepower, turning four-blade Hamilton Standard Hydromatic propellers of 15-ft 2-in diameter. This combination easily coped with a gross weight exceeding 76,000 lb in the P-2E version – considerably heavier than any B-17. [*Philip Wallick*]

ABOVE LEFT Parked on the same ramp as the Aero Union P-2 Tanker 01, this P-2H belongs to another operator, Evergreen Air Tankers, which operates from Missoula, Montana. In this head-on shot the P-2's jet pods stand out well; each contains a Westinghouse J34 turbojet of 3400 lb thrust. They permit operation at increased weight and make a big difference to take-off and initial climb. The aircraft was converted at the Evergreen Air Center, part of the Marana Air Park complex in Arizona. [*Philip Wallick*]

LEFT The P-2's span of 103 ft 10 in in its original form is actually slightly greater than the span of a B-17, but the high aspect-ratio wing has considerably less area. Note the 'sawn off' tail where the MAD stinger used to be. Sadly, the market could not support a totally new purpose-designed tanker other than the Canadair CL-215, so conversions are likely to rule the Western states for the rest of the century. [*Philip Wallick*]

ABOVE In this view the P-2H's jet pods are clearly seen, as is the capacious payload tank – one of the biggest in current use. The P-2 is not a cheap aircraft to maintain, but it is one of the best fire-bomber tankers so far to become available. [*Philip Wallick*]

ABOVE This Evergreen P-2 has the operator's handsome white livery with green cheatline. It also retains the original transparent nose, but (like most other P-2 tankers) has lost its original wingtip fuel tanks. As a tanker the P-2 can be flown solo, though workload is rather higher than with most other types. [*Philip Wallick*]

LOCKHEED
Hercules

RIGHT Markair's L-100-30 N107AK after arriving on Unalakleet's gravel runway from Anchorage International via Nome on a July evening in 1986.

BELOW On top of the world – well, quite close. N107AK's flight engineer invited Karl-Heinz Morawietz to take the Alaskan air from the L-100's roof garden.
[*Photographs by Karl-Heinz Morawietz/Jörg Weier*]

LOCKHEED HERCULES

Formerly known as Alaska International Air, Markair
operates a mixed fleet of Boeing 737 and Lockheed
L-100 Hercules on scheduled passenger and cargo
services throughout Alaska and to Seattle,
Washington. [*Karl-Heinz Morawietz/Jörg Weier*]

BELOW New name, old colours. When operated by Alaska International N108AK was a familiar visitor to European airports, but Markair confine their operations to Alaska and the US mainland. Lockheed has sold 109 L-100 civil freighter versions of the ubiquitous C-130.
[*Karl-Heinz Morawietz/Jörg Weier*]

LEFT Sun screens and Ray-Bans are needed as characteristic Alaskan late evening light floods the spacious flight deck through the L-100's 15 cockpit windows. [*Karl-Heinz Morawietz/Jörg Weier*]

LEFT Markair has three of these L-100-30 stretched versions of the commercial Hercules, each with a maximum payload of 51,054 lb.
[*Karl-Heinz Morawietz/Jörg Weier*]

ABOVE N522SJ is a Lockheed L-382E Hercules operated by Southern Air Transport from their heavily guarded and fenced ramp on the northern perimeter of Miami International Airport. SAT specializes in the movement of outsize cargo as well as contract and ad hoc freight serves for commercial clients and the US and other governments, using a mixed fleet of Boeing 707s and Hercules.
[*Austin J. Brown/Mark R. Wagner*]

LOCKHEED HERCULES

Land of the midnight sun: Markair's N107AK at
20,000 feet, departing from Unalakleet just after the
witching hour. On a few summer days in the Alaskan
north the sun shines right around the clock.
[*Karl-Heinz Morawietz/Jörg Weier*]